I Write What is Right!
Cursive Edition

This book belongs to:

Proverbs 22:6
Train up a child in the way he
should go, and when he is old he
will not depart from it.

able

Numbers 13:30
Then Caleb quieted the people before Moses, and said, "Let us go up at once and take possession, for we are well able to overcome it."

I am well able.

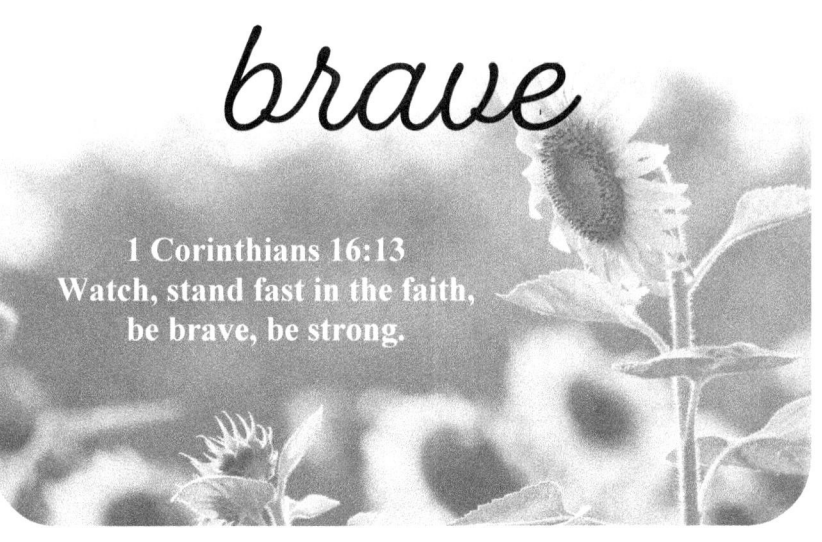

brave

1 Corinthians 16:13
Watch, stand fast in the faith,
be brave, be strong.

I am brave.

conqueror

Romans 8:37
**Yet in all these things we are
more than conquerors through
Him who loved us.**

I am more than a conqueror.

diligent

Proverbs 12:24
The hand of the diligent will rule, But the lazy man will be put to forced labor.

I am diligent.

elect

Colossians 3:12
Therefore, as the elect of
God, holy and beloved, put
on tender mercies, kindness,
humility, meekness, longsuffering;

I am the elect of God.

forgiven

Ephesians 4:32
And be kind to one another, tenderhearted, forgiving one another, even as God in Christ forgave you.

I am forgiven.

grace

John 1:16
And of His fullness we have all
received, and grace for grace.

I have grace.

hope

Psalm 31:24
Be of good courage,
And He shall strengthen your heart,
All you who hope in the Lord.

I have hope.

indescribable

2 Corinthians 9:15
Thanks be to God for His indescribable gift!

I have His indescribable gift.

joy

John 15:11
"These things I have spoken to you,
that My joy may remain in you, and
that your joy may be full."

I have joy.

kind

Romans 12:10
Be kindly affectionate to one another
with brotherly love, in honor giving
preference to one another;

I am kind.

love

1 John 4:7
Beloved, let us love one another, for love is of God; and everyone who loves is born of God and knows God.

I show love.

mind

1 Corinthians 2:16
For "who has known the mind of
the Lord that he may instruct Him?"
But we have the mind of Christ.

I have the mind of Christ.

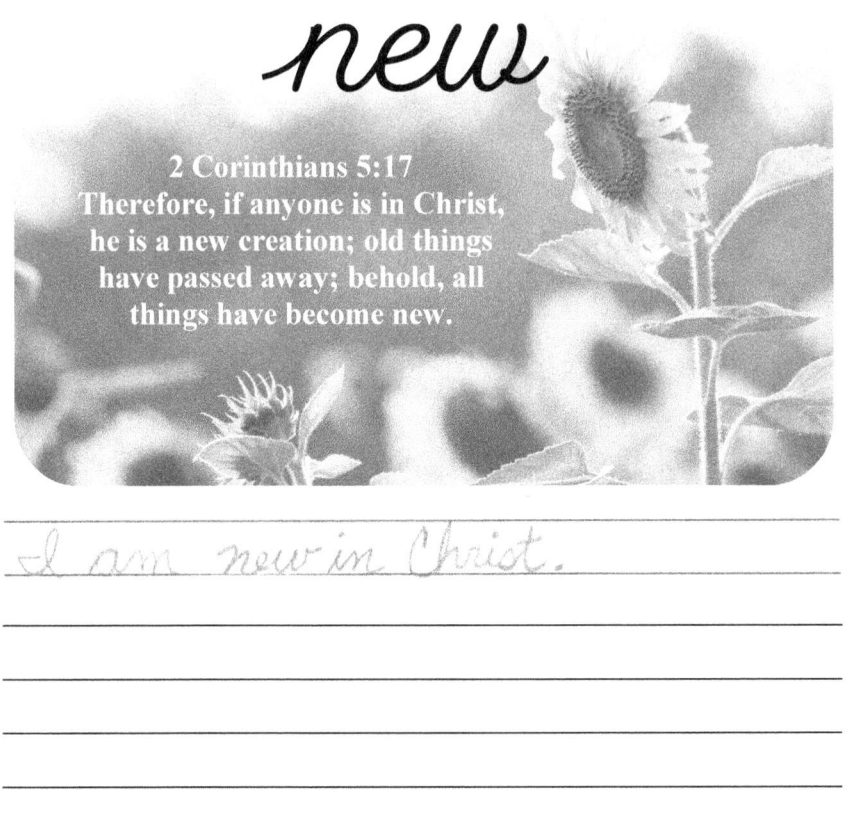

new

2 Corinthians 5:17
Therefore, if anyone is in Christ,
he is a new creation; old things
have passed away; behold, all
things have become new.

I am new in Christ.

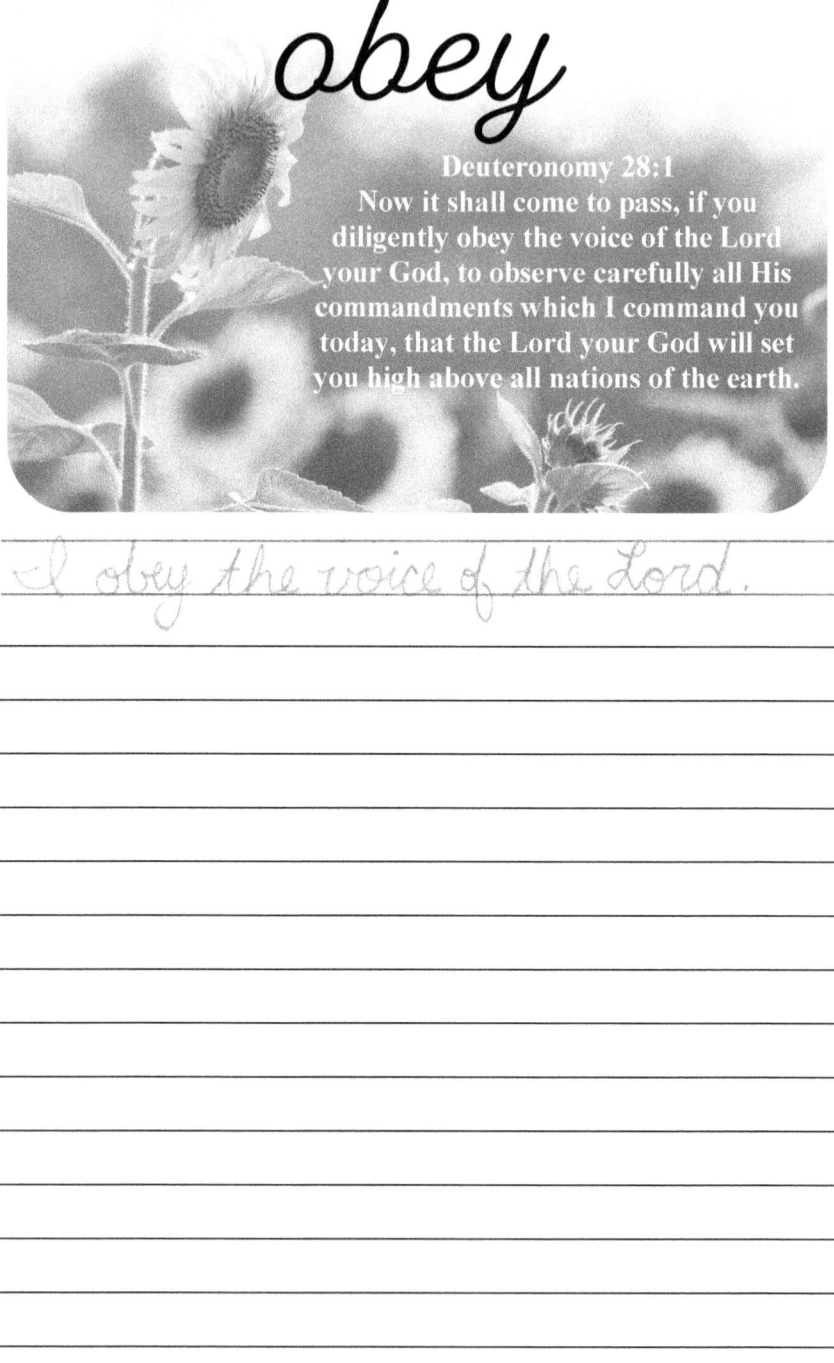

obey

Deuteronomy 28:1
Now it shall come to pass, if you diligently obey the voice of the Lord your God, to observe carefully all His commandments which I command you today, that the Lord your God will set you high above all nations of the earth.

I obey the voice of the Lord.

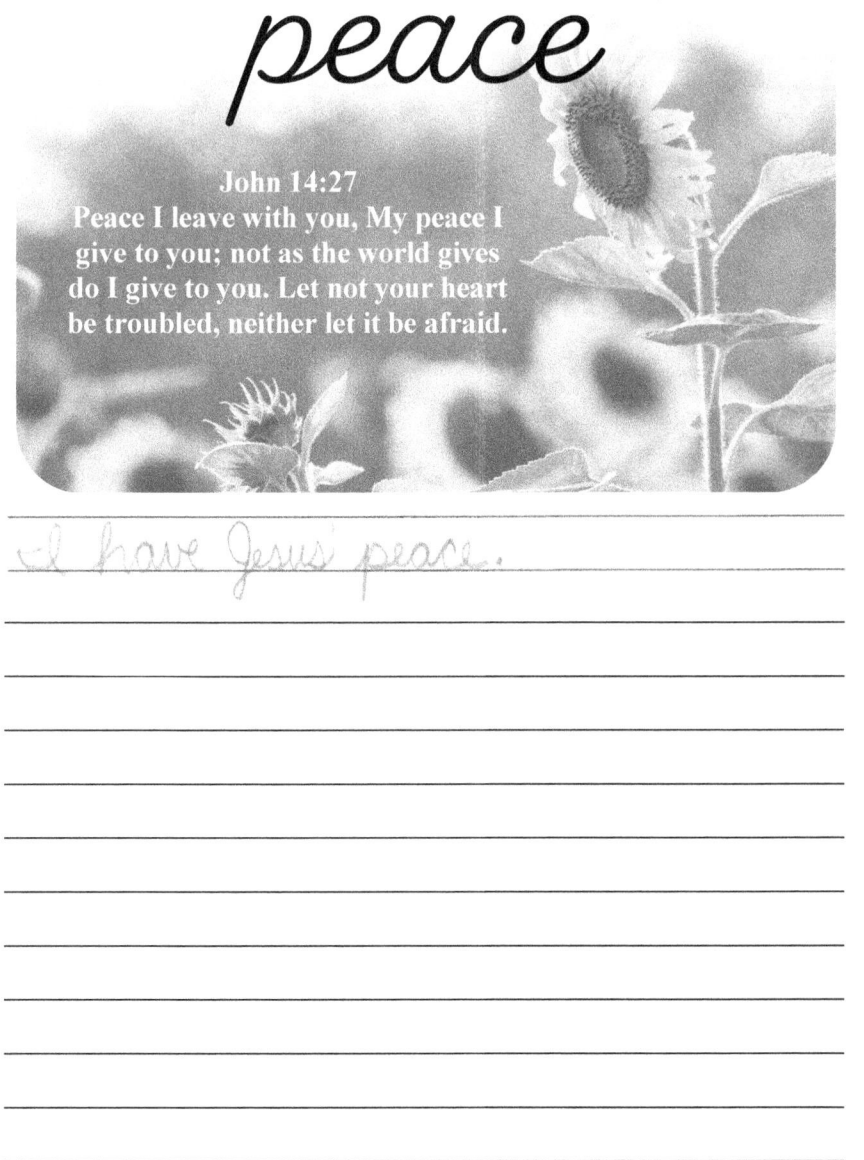

peace

John 14:27
Peace I leave with you, My peace I
give to you; not as the world gives
do I give to you. Let not your heart
be troubled, neither let it be afraid.

I have Jesus' peace.

quench

1 Thessalonians 5:19
Do not quench the Spirit

I must not quench the Holy Spirit.

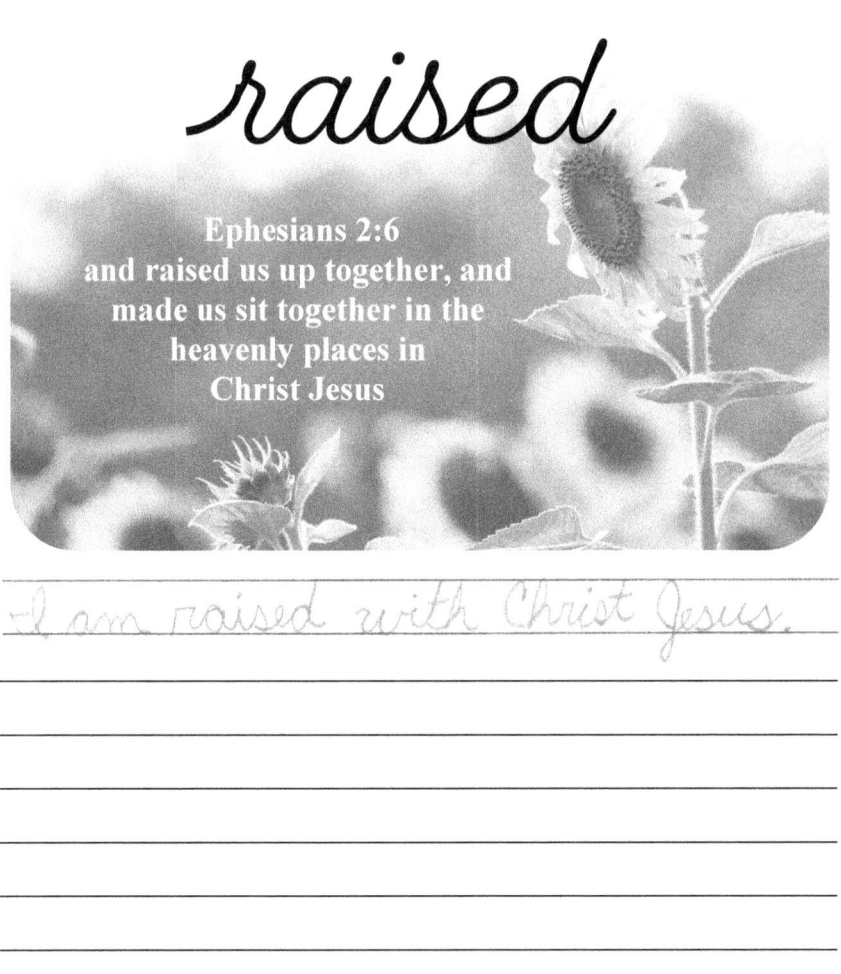

raised

Ephesians 2:6
and raised us up together, and
made us sit together in the
heavenly places in
Christ Jesus

I am raised with Christ Jesus.

submit

James 4:7
Therefore submit to God.
Resist the devil and
he will flee from you.

I submit to God.

taught

John 14:26
But the Helper, the Holy Spirit,
whom the Father will send in My
name, He will teach you all things,
and bring to your remembrance
all things that I said to you.

I am taught by the Holy Spirit.

understand

Luke 24:45
And He opened their understanding, that they might comprehend the Scriptures.

I am able to understand mysteries.

victorious

1 Corinthians 15:57
But thanks be to God,
who gives us the victory
through our Lord Jesus Christ

I am victorious.

wonder

Psalm 71:7
I have become as a wonder
to many, But You are
my strong refuge.

I am a wonder.

exalt

Psalm 46:10
Be still, and know that I am God;
I will be exalted among the
nations, I will be exalted
in the earth!

I exalt the Lord.

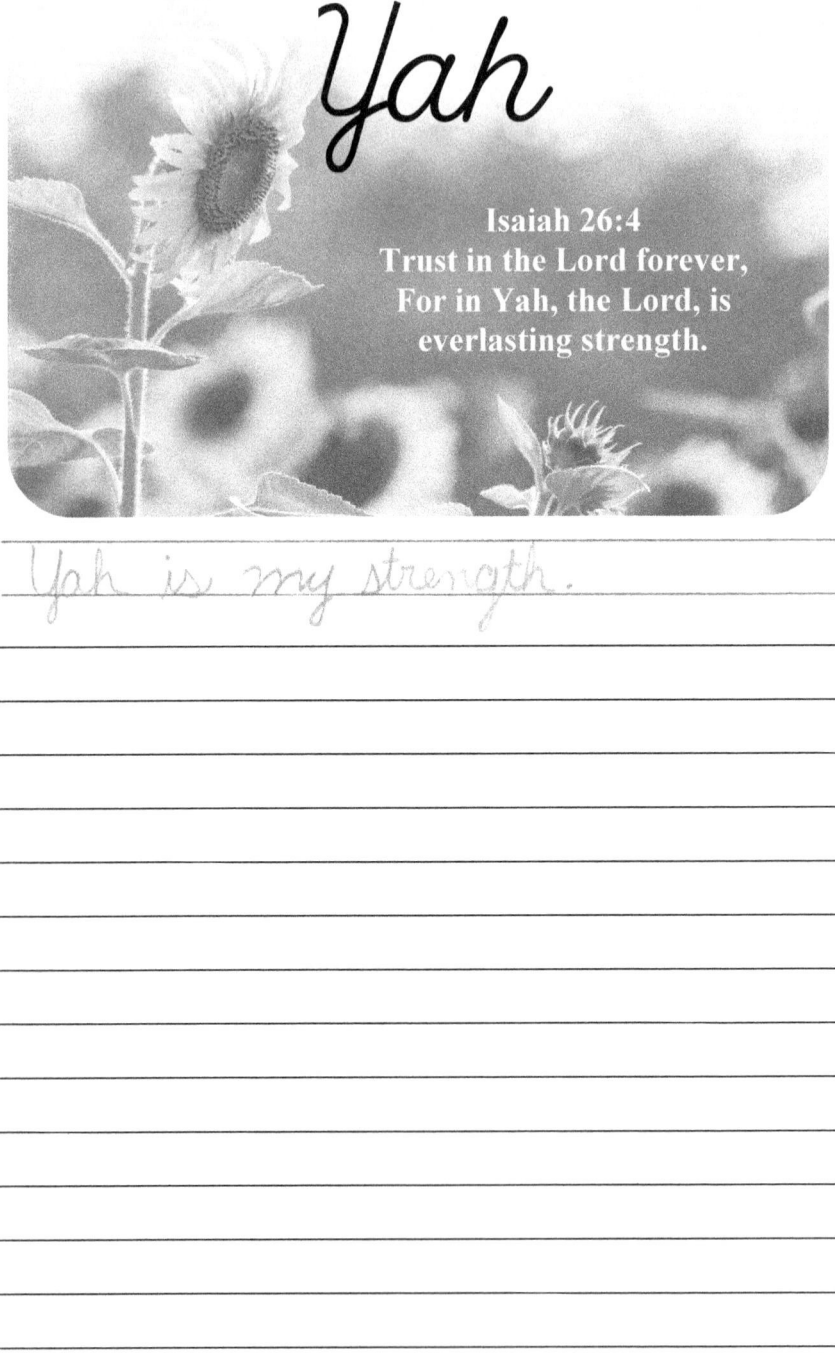

Yah

Isaiah 26:4
Trust in the Lord forever,
For in Yah, the Lord, is
everlasting strength.

Yah is my strength.

zealous

Proverbs 23:17
Do not let your heart envy sinners,
But be zealous for the fear of the
Lord all the day;

I am zealous for the Lord.

Who is Jesus?

Jesus is the Son of God.
He was sent to the earth to
pay the ransom for our sin.
What was broken, is now fixed.

Jesus teaches us how to build
the kingdom of heaven, by
activating the kingdom of God,
inside each of us. He also teaches
us to anticipate the glory of
heaven, which is every
believer's eternal home.

Because of Jesus' great love for
us, He paid our sin debt in full
with His precious blood on the
cross. All of us who believe and
accept His gift, enter into right
standing with God and
are heirs of His Kingdom.

You are LOVED.
You were created for great
purpose. You are forgiven of all
wrongdoing. Ask God for help and
guidance each day. Know the Holy
Spirit lives in you and will
comfort, teach, heal,
and empower you.

In Jesus Name,
Amen

Mission: To Proclaim Transformation and Truth

Publisher: Transformed Publishing, Cocoa, FL
Website: www.transformedpublishing.com
Email: transformedpublishing@gmail.com

ISBN: 978-1-953241-32-0

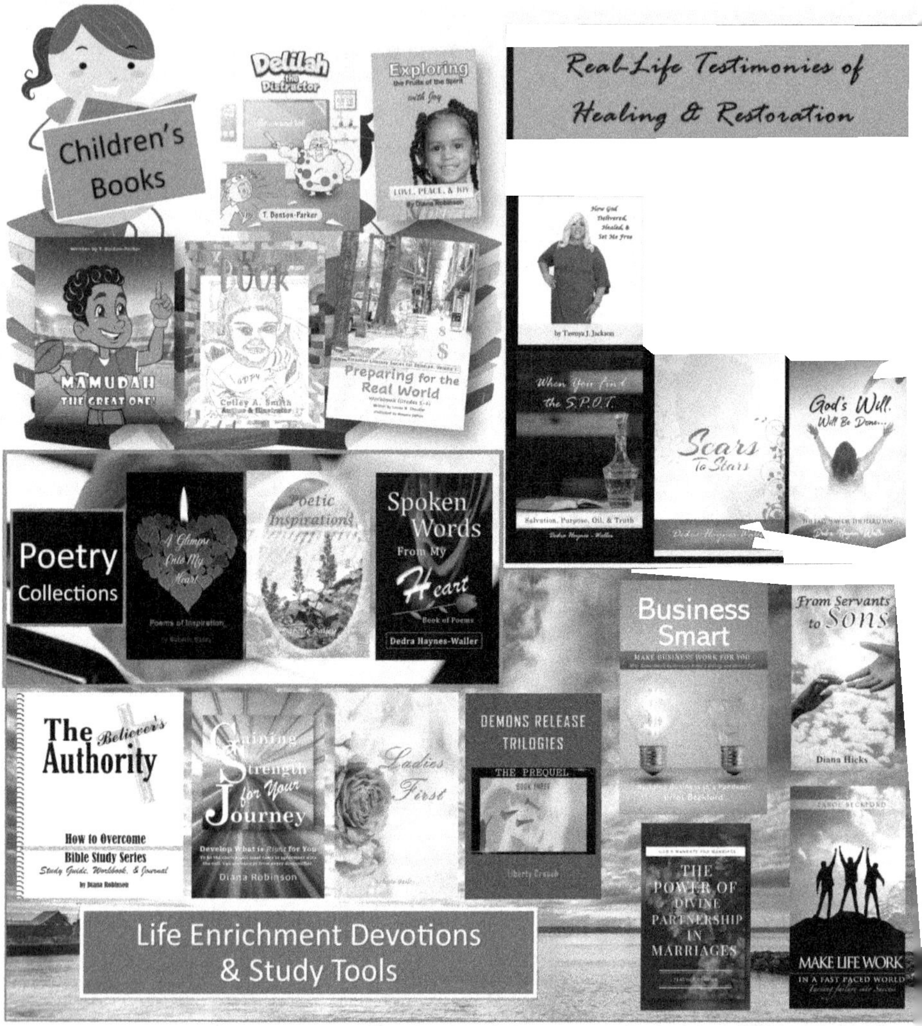
Children's Books
Delilah the Distractor
Exploring the Fruits of the Spirit with Joy
LOVE, PEACE, & JOY
T. Benton-Parker
Real-Life Testimonies of Healing & Restoration
How God Delivered, Healed, & Set Me Free
by Teresa J. Jackson
MAMUDAH THE GREAT ONE!
Colley A. Smith
Preparing for the Real World
When You Find the S.P.O.T.
Salvation, Purpose, Oil, & Truth
Scars To Stars
God's Will, Will Be Done...
Poetry Collections
A Glimpse Into My Heart
Poems of Inspiration
Poetic Inspirations
Spoken Words From My Heart
Book of Poems
Dedra Haynes-Waller
Business Smart
From Servants to Sons
Diana Hicks
The Believer's Authority
How to Overcome
Bible Study Series
Study Guide, Workbook, & Journal
by Diana Robinson
Gaining Strength for Your Journey
Develop What is Right for You
Diana Robinson
Ladies First
DEMONS RELEASE TRILOGIES
THE PREQUEL
THE POWER OF DIVINE PARTNERSHIP IN MARRIAGES
MAKE LIFE WORK
IN A FAST PACED WORLD
Life Enrichment Devotions & Study Tools

www.ingramcontent.com/pod-product-compliance
Lightning Source LLC
Chambersburg PA
CBHW070957120626
46546CB00004B/1665